"Champions aren't made in gyms. Champions are made from something they have deep inside them - a desire, a dream, a vision. They have to have the skill and the will. But the will must be stronger than the skill."

Muhammad Ali

Ask the Dojo Doctor

I'm a beginner in MMA, and I often experience pain in my wrists during training. What can I do to prevent this?

Wrist pain is a common issue for beginners in martial arts. To prevent this, make sure you're using proper technique when punching or blocking. Keep your wrist straight and aligned with your forearm. You can also perform wrist strengthening exercises, such as wrist curls and reverse wrist curls, to build strength and stability.

Additionally, consider using wrist wraps or supports during training to provide extra protection and support. If the pain persists or worsens, consult with your instructor or a medical professional.

I've been training in martial arts for a while, but I feel like I've hit a plateau in my progress. How can I continue to improve?

Plateaus are a normal part of any martial arts journey. To break through and continue improving, try the following:

1. Set specific goals: identify areas where you want to improve and set measurable goals to work towards.
2. Vary your training: incorporate different drills, techniques, and training methods to challenge your body and mind in new ways.
3. Cross-train: explore other martial arts styles or complementary practices like yoga or weightlifting to develop a well-rounded skill set.
4. Analyze your performance: record yourself during training or sparring and review the footage to identify areas for improvement.
5. Seek feedback: ask your instructor or training partners for constructive criticism and advice on how to refine your technique.

Remember, consistent practice and a growth mindset are key to long-term progress

After a considerable break I have returned to training at a local dojo. I was previously a black belt and the new style allow me to wear my black belt to class which I thought was a good thing because I feel I am too old to go back to being a white belt. The trouble is this new style is way more complex than my previous style and I am really feeling out of place. What can I do to catch up without becoming a liability in every class I attend?

Returning to martial arts after a break can be challenging, especially when joining a new style that is more complex than your previous one. Here are some tips to help you catch up and avoid feeling like a liability in class:

1. Discuss your situation with your instructor, letting them know about your previous experience and your desire to catch up. They may be able to provide you with additional guidance, resources, or private lessons to help you bridge the gap.
2. Even though you're wearing a black belt, don't hesitate to spend extra time practicing the fundamental techniques of the new style. Mastering the basics will provide a solid foundation for learning more advanced techniques.
3. After each class, write down the techniques, drills, and concepts you learned. Review your notes between classes to reinforce your understanding and identify areas where you need more practice.
4. Dedicate time to practicing techniques and forms on your own. This will allow you to progress at your own pace and build muscle memory.
5. Don't be afraid to ask your instructor or advanced students for clarification or advice when you're unsure about a technique or concept. Most martial artists are happy to help others learn and grow.
6. Learning a new style takes time, so don't be too hard on yourself if you feel like you're not progressing as quickly as you'd like. Celebrate your small victories and improvements along the way.

Everyone in class is there to learn and grow, regardless of rank. By consistently putting in the effort and maintaining a positive attitude, you'll soon find yourself catching up and contributing to the dojo's community.

Dear Readers,

In this edition of Martial Arts Magazine Australia, we delve into the fascinating world of mindset and how it influences our martial arts journey. As practitioners, we often focus on physical techniques and skills, but the true essence of martial arts lies in the development of our inner selves.

The concepts of ego and id, as described by Sigmund Freud, play a significant role in shaping our mindset. The ego represents our conscious self, while the id represents our primitive, instinctual drives. In martial arts, we must learn to balance these two aspects of our psyche.

When the ego dominates, we may fall prey to arrogance, self-doubt, or the need to prove ourselves. This can lead to overconfidence, unnecessary risk-taking, and a lack of respect for our training partners. When the id takes over, we may give in to aggression, anger, or fear, clouding our judgment and hindering our progress.

The key to success in martial arts lies in developing a mindset that harmonises the ego and the id. We must cultivate humility, self-awareness, and emotional control. By acknowledging our strengths and weaknesses, we open ourselves up to continuous learning and growth. By managing our instinctual responses, we can maintain focus, discipline, and respect in our training.

Embracing a growth mindset is crucial. We must view challenges as opportunities for improvement rather than threats to our ego. Every setback is a chance to learn, adapt, and come back stronger. By fostering a love for the process of learning and self-discovery, we can find joy and fulfillment in our martial arts practice.

Remember, the true opponent lies within. Our mindset, ego, and id are the forces we must confront and master on our martial arts journey. By developing self-awareness, humility, and emotional control, we can unlock our full potential and embody the true spirit of martial arts.

Stay curious, stay humble, and keep training!
Until next time, Happy reading.

Yours sincerely,

Vanessa McKay

All content published in MAMA (Marital Arts Magazine Australia), including articles, images, and other media, is the property of the magazine and is protected by copyright law. The author retains the copyright to their individual work, but by submitting their work to MAMA, they grant the magazine an exclusive, perpetual, and irrevocable license to publish and distribute their work in all formats, including print, digital, and online media. No part of MAMA may be reproduced, distributed, or transmitted in any form or by any means, including photocopying, recording, or other electronic or mechanical methods, without the prior written permission of the magazine.

MAMA respects the intellectual property rights of others and expects its contributors and readers to do the same. If you believe that your copyrighted work has been used in a way that constitutes copyright infringement, please contact MAMA immediately. Additionally, any use of MAMA trademarks, including the magazine's name and logo, without prior written authorization from the magazine, is prohibited.

MAMA strives to showcase original and unique content, and as such, does not accept any submissions that have been previously published or that are under consideration by other publications. By submitting their work to MAWA Magazine, the author confirms that their work is original and has not been published or submitted elsewhere.

In addition, MAMA reserves the right to edit all submissions for grammar, style, and clarity, and to reject any submission that does not adhere to the magazine's standards or guidelines. The magazine also reserves the right to remove or modify any content that is deemed inappropriate or offensive, at its sole discretion.

MAMA acknowledges and respects the rights of all individuals and groups and will not publish any content that promotes hate speech, discrimination, or any form of violence. The magazine also respects the privacy of its contributors and readers and will not share or sell any personal information to third parties without prior written consent. By submitting their work to MAMA, the author agrees to abide by these copyright specifics and to grant the magazine the rights outlined in this statement. The author also certifies that their work is original and does not infringe on the rights of any third party. MAMA reserves the right to modify these copyright specifics at any time without prior notice.

If you have any questions or concerns regarding these copyright specifics, please contact MAMA at info@martialartsmagazineaustralia.com

CONTENTS

The Dojo Doctor	5
Event Horizon & Elastic Time	7
Harnessing Traditional Martial Arts...	10
Finding the Motivation to Train...	16
Helping Others in the dojo	19
Karate Self Esteem Ego & Id	21
Powerful Yoga Fusion & MA	24
Post Training Recipes	33
The French Disconnection	37
Matayoshi Kobudo	40
Combat Analysis	44
Offensive Action Toward Second dan	46
Karate No Rinrir	48
Mastering Kata	51

e secret to unlocking your full potential through the power of "event theory" – where time ceases to exist, and you become one with the moment.

Event Horizon & Elastic Time
by Benjamin Ward

In the vast expanse of space, a black hole signifies a state of no time, wherein all matter enclosed within is forever confined, unable to escape. Light itself is confined within, resulting in its black appearance. The region around a black hole is known as the event horizon. The region encompassing the black hole establishes a boundary where time, in its conventional form, becomes nonexistent.

I started my martial arts training as a 13-year-old and quickly became engrossed in it, which led to idolizing Jackie Chan and Bruce Lee. Me and my mate from karate class would stay up all night eating pizza and watching their movies or reruns of Mortal Kombat, the tv series to find techniques that were showy which we could practice in the backyard the next day. This fascination with 'the Bruce' led me to follow in his footsteps and I started to incorporate cross training into my regime.

This mostly involved cross country running. Six kilometres along a track I had measured using the odometer in my dad's car. When I went on these runs, I would swear at myself to keep going, motivating myself in my head or out loud. At a certain point into the run, I seemed to lose my awareness of anything but the moment and the next thing I knew I was at the end of the run and twenty minutes had passed seemingly instantaneously. I had exited the running experience.

There seemed to be a great deal of energy produced from these runs and my training. I felt more energised at my part time job and at school following training. But the interesting thing was that 'no-time' occurred during my run. I experienced the same thing when I took up meditation and, following a guided meditation one day, I ascended into the clouds of visualisation to experience a feeling of ecstasy and for a while there was no time then to.

Circle back to 23 years later and I am writing this article because in an introduction to sports and exercise class at university, I had a conversation with a guy around my age about warming up the body. He told me with great enthusiasm that he knows he is warmed up and 'into' his workout when he starts jogging, skipping or running prelims and his leg muscles really hurt but eventually his legs stop hurting without him realising until a lightbulb moment of realisation occurs. We discussed circumspectly that it was blood flow but we both knew better as we exchanged knowing looks.

This can be explained by what is roughly called 'event theory' in that going into any event, be it a session of exercise, a drinking session, to read a book or basically anything where you try to live in the moment, beyond that beginning bit where you must invest energy and motivation into it. Event theory says that if you invest enough energy and motivation into something there comes a point where you cross into the event horizon (from black hole science) where it no longer takes any more self-generated motivation to keep going and the event generates its own energy. To understand this, one has to visualize the event as an entity (just like a black hole or a thing) and the participant is going into it. Into the run; the event; motivational speech being attended; the class; the housework; the job. The event starts to self-generate and there is no-time for a period. Often when the person has left the event's energy and exited the other side of the event horizon, they notice in an a-ha kind of moment and realize their actions and thoughts require motivation and deliverance again.

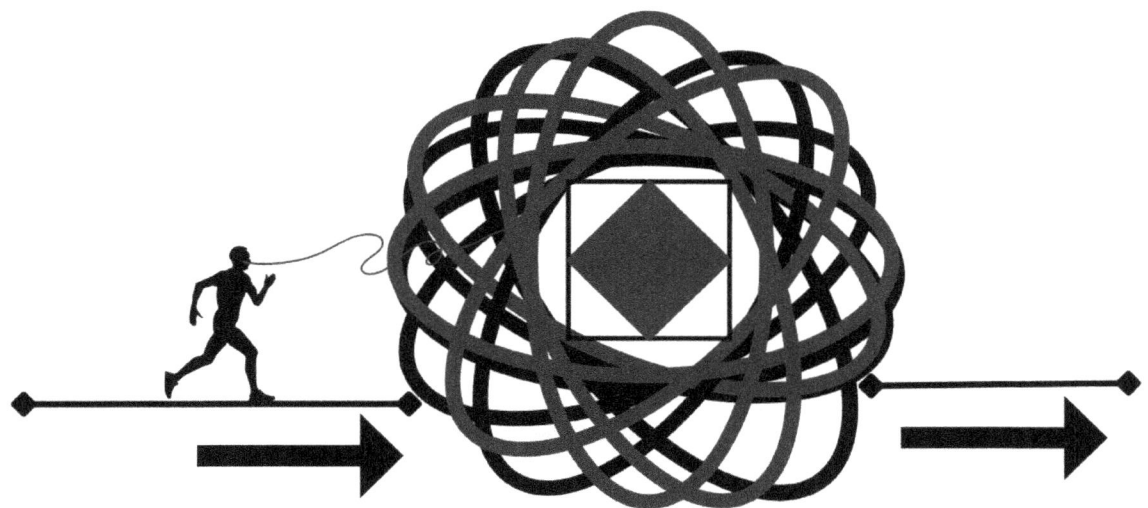

This theory explains a lot of martial arts concepts, like 'one shot', 'one hit' or 'ippon' where one strike guarantees victory. It is said the technique exists in the mind before its execution and victory precedes the winner. And, 'mushin' or no mind is about getting lost in the moment, where a fight can be perceived as both short or long, and where spontaneity and pure reflexes of the spirit exist. Having a sixth sense to detect attackers on either side is all about the 'meaningful coincidences' that happen during high-energy events. These concepts in karate are a blending of spirit and tactics. And all of them discuss time as being non-linear. The Japanese were well aware of this phenomenon through their martial arts training and had specialised the occurrences into methodical practice for experience of what event theory says is entering the entity of an event and what is possible there.

Interestingly, as just mentioned, meaningful coincidences seem to surround high energy events aside from just the relative time distinctions and generating of motivational energy. A thing that happens around these events is meeting people and going places and finding things and revelations of links that energy of the same quality as the event reaches back into the past from it and into the future.

This can be explained by the modern way of quantum physics, string theory. Event theory simply describes the links of the event to the synchronicities as another dimension in a different state of time where all the meaningful coincidences come from a common point which we localize as being the entity of the event. String theory talks of compactification, and calabi-yau manifolds and fluxes and branes. All of which are complex forms of explaining how something we can't quite understand, and measure is shaping occurrences in the historical world. Here in the historical world we found the Cartesian dimensions of x,y and z and of course our civilizations' life long struggle with time and unexplained phenomena which we have decided science is the answer to. However, Japanese Karateka of centuries ago have always talked about the sixth sense and who can forget the ancient Japanese Shintō practice of going up a mountain top to escape the dimensions of daily life. And how does one explain the powers of a Kame or God?

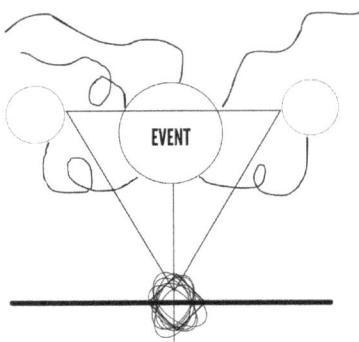

These events contain no time and don't just house our experiences but exist on levels we aren't aware of. So how does a middle-aged athlete or karateka implement this knowledge into his technique practice without involving stimuli into the practice such as substances which affect the experience or results of events such as alcohol for example, and maintain meditation and purification? Which admittedly must be done to their best ability or in certain periods of fasting, as most intermediate humans have one vice or another. The answer comes from psychology and the study of motivation.

It is also relative to third dan black belt practice in that confronting multiple attackers involves a training of thoughts and behaviour for a well rehearsed grading and an ability to apply this to real life situations. This requires flipping a switch into victory preceding the winner. Second dan black belt also for its consistency of training required develops a notion of real world responsibilities through simplification of the training into advanced conditioning while also maintaining a family or a job or a mortgage. Psychology tells us we must have conditions in our life but also allow ourselves to live in the moment. Psychology basically professes balanced living as one of its great steeples.

It is different for everyone but finding responsibility and consistency with one's conditions of survival, health, safety and well-being is needed. That allows one to enter events of experience where no-time exists and as is the Japanese way to be a master of many things. Mastery occurs through these immersive experiences.

Interestingly, event theory has a take on this too. It says that the law of entropy, which is the structured energy held together in a system, releases energy when it breaks down. Like in a pond where the frogs stop eating the flies so the flies multiply. The entropy that occurs in events is with our sense of time what we think we are capable of doing versus what we achieve.

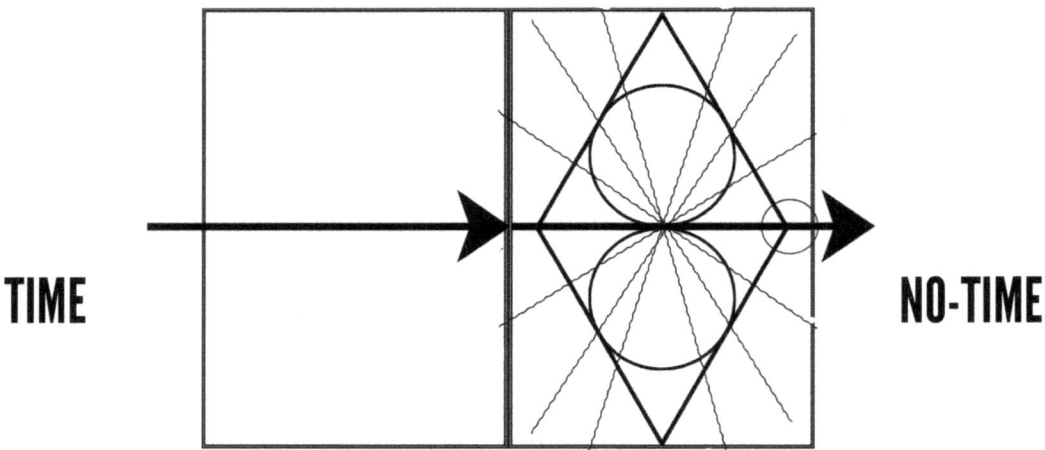

TIME   **NO-TIME**

Realizing we are capable of more than we thought at the beginning of something is breaking down a held belief. And this explains the euphoria that exists from finishing a workout, learning new things, or a very unexpected experience. The Japanese describe it as an awareness of the waves which form thought, which allows the sixth sense.

But maybe the final question event theory puts to the reader is does this breaking down of one's sentimental energies affect the world rather than just being able to be perceived? Are these meaningful coincidences coming from a place of meaning which we just don't know how to measure yet? Is there a spiritual aspect to the no-time we experience in training and is it being in line with the Kame?

HARNESSING TRADITIONAL MARTIAL ARTS FOR MODERN SELF-DEFENCE
by Connor Charlton

Brazilian Jiu Jitsu (BJJ) has become a global phenomenon and is one of the fastest growing martial arts on the planet. Jiu-Jitsu's journey to Brazil involved a fascinating exchange of knowledge. Judokas, masters of Judo (which itself developed from Jujutsu and even older arts), like Mitsuyo Maeda, Soshihiro Satake, and Geo Omori, travelled extensively. Their journeys across Asia, Europe, and the Americas exposed them to catch wrestling techniques. These grapplers eventually found themselves in Brazil, where they incorporated these new learnings into their Judo teachings, influencing students and competing in professional wrestling matches.

At one of these wrestling matches was a teenage Carlos Gracie. Carlos had been brought to the match by his father Gastão, who owned and ran the circus which hosted the match. Gastão feared Carlos lacked discipline, and it was his belief that Mitsuyo's Jiu Jitsu would rectify this behavioural issue and was proven correct. Carlos dedicated his life to the art and his four brothers would train alongside Maeda.

Because of his small stature and past medical issues, his younger brother Helio Gracie had some trouble using some methods. He concentrated on creating methods that leveraged time, leverage, and skill rather than just brute force to combat this. He experimented with different poses, such as the trunk stance, which wasn't often utilised in judo. Gracie's study of the trunk, or dō-osae posture, would be very beneficial and eventually lead to the guard position, which gave them the advantage over grapplers of other styles.

What separates Brazilian Jiu Jitsu from Judo is that it puts a much greater emphasis on 'ne-waza', or ground fighting. Judo, particularly in its competition form, puts a lot of focus on its standing or tachi-waza techniques.

Although there would be other key figures in the art's development like Luis Franca, Oswaldo Fadda, it would be the Gracies who would bring the art to the wider world, opening schools in the US and Europe, with family members such as Royce and Rickson showcasing its effectiveness in the early UFC and Pride events. Between the rise of Mixed Martial Arts as a sport, high-profile comedians like Joe Rogan and actors like Keanu Reeves endorsing its effectiveness, the growth of no-gi grappling competition, 'the gentle art' has experienced explosive flourish over the last three decades.

Losing the Effectiveness

Despite BJJ's growth in popularity, there has been some debate about its evolution. Similar to Judo, the martial art from which many of its techniques originate, BJJ has arguably become more sport-oriented. Whilst it is exciting to see a new sport with big personalities like Craig Jones and Gordon Ryan make waves on the global stage, there are a number of downsides which come from the sportification of any art. Brazilian Jiu Jitsu is effective because students develop their skills through live-sparring or "rolling". Akin to the randori practice found in Judo, rolling is a great form of pressure-testing technical abilities, but it does have some limitations.

As the art itself contains no strikes, the vast majority of competitions do not permit them and, as a result, tournament-focused clubs might fail to teach ways to defend these attacks.

Additionally, these clubs can put too much focus on techniques which are designed to score points within competition rule sets, which aren't as applicable to real life combat scenarios. For instance, whilst Helio's exploration of the guard position has allowed BJJ practitioners to overcome larger and stronger opponents, using it and retaining it in self-defence situations can leave you prone to attacks from multiple assailants. When attacked by a group, you will want to get back to your feet and make as quick an exit as possible. Knowing when to go to the ground and when to stay on your feet is an important part of self-defence.

Although it's far from a universal problem, competition training can give some practitioners a false sense of security for environments outside of the mats.Fighting on glass-covered street-cobbles, where anything can be a makeshift weapon is a lot different to soft gym mats.

Standard Brazilian Jiu Jitsu training also doesn't tend to teach important aspects of self-defence, such as handling attackers with weapons, or developing a keen sense of awareness.

Combatting the Loss of Effectiveness

To enhance BJJ's all-round effectiveness, there are a number of techniques and practices found in older martial arts, particularly Japanese Jujutsu, which can be of enormous benefit. One of the most important things is mindset and awareness. The mindset of self-defence, including situational awareness and de-escalation techniques, is inherent to many older martial arts traditions.Regardless of which art you train, should you find yourself having to defend yourself, your primary goal should be to subdue threats and escape safety, rather than dominate, humiliate and injure.

One of the elements of Brazilian Jiu Jitsu which makes it effective is the use of live sparring or rolling sessions to assess your strengths and weaknesses. Understanding your limitations is crucial in self-defence, and will keep your focus on de-escalation or escape.

Sparring will allow you to test these techniques, which have come from older martial arts.

Hip Throw (O-Goshi):
Sometimes Brazilian Jiu Jitsu practitioners will eschew stand up grappling practice and proceed straight to ground-fighting techniques.However, in order to utilise ground-fighting techniques, you need get the fight to the ground and take downs, trips and throws are the way to do it. One such throw is the o-goshi or hip throw. The hip throw, which has its roots in classical Jujutsu and Judo, is unbalancing your opponent and throwing them to the ground by using your hip and leverage. It works well in self-defence scenarios where you have to take out an attacker fast.

Armbar (Ude-Hishigi-Juji-Gatame):
The armbar is a traditional submission move from Judo that entails pinning your opponent's arm between your knees and applying pressure with your hips to hyperextend the elbow joint. This manoeuvre is adaptable and can be used to stop an assailant or block a grab or punch.

Rear Naked Choke (Hadaka Jime):
The rear naked choke is another submission method that was taken from Judo and has roots which stretch back to ancient battlefield grappling techniques. It entails putting your arm around your opponent's neck and applying pressure to stop the blood supply to the brain. It's a very powerful tactic to subdue an adversary without doing them any lasting damage when it is used correctly.

Joint Locks (Kansetsu-Waza):
There are dozens of joint locks, or variations of these locks which can submit an opponent. Various joint locks, such as the kimura lock (ude-garami) and Americana (Ude Juji Jime) have their origins in traditional Japanese Jujutsu. The kimura which appears in the teachings of jujutsu schools like the Kitun-ryu utilises leverage and body mechanics to isolate and potentially dislocate the shoulder joint. Whilst the Americana can be found in the teachings of the Tenshin Shinyo-ryu, Jujutsu school is a shoulder joint which hyper extends the shoulder. Both techniques can be effective for smaller individuals looking to control or incapacitate larger opponents.

Strikes from the Guard Position:
While BJJ primarily focuses on grappling, it also incorporates strikes that have roots in older martial arts. From the guard position, techniques like elbow strikes, palm strikes, and hammer fists can be utilised to create distance or deter an attacker.

Scissor Sweep (Kani Basami):
Derived from Judo, the scissor sweep involves using your legs to off-balance your opponent and sweep them onto their back. It's an effective technique for self-defence situations where you find yourself on the ground and need to quickly reverse the position.

Shrimping
This fundamental movement in BJJ involves using your hips and back to create space and escape from dangerous positions on the ground. Shrimping is a core concept in jujutsu and other grappling arts, allowing practitioners to manoeuvrer and regain control during groundwork.

Frame Control
Maintaining a strong frame with your arms and legs to prevent your opponent from controlling you is a crucial self-defence concept emphasised in BJJ. Frame control techniques can be traced back to older grappling arts, where maintaining a dominant position and preventing grappling holds is essential.

These techniques highlight the practical applications of BJJ for self-defence while acknowledging their historical origins in older martial arts. By mastering these techniques, practitioners can effectively defend themselves in real-world situations while honouring the rich heritage of martial arts.

Other Self Defence Principles

Train in both gi and no-gi
In BJJ, training in both gi and no-gi offers complimentary techniques for self-defence. While no-gi training focuses on body mechanics and flexibility for circumstances without clothing for grabs, gi training refines throws and grips using the kimono. This adaptability, which is reminiscent of earlier martial arts ideas, equips practitioners for a range of self-defence situations, independent of the attacker's clothes or the time of year.

Incorporate Striking and Striking Defence
While BJJ primarily focuses on grappling, older Japanese martial arts like Jujutsu included striking techniques as well. By incorporating striking and striking defence into their training, BJJ practitioners develop a greater understanding of distance and timing management, which can be particularly important when facing armed assailants. Older martial arts such as traditional Japanese jujutsu and kenjutsu (swordsmanship) have some techniques involved. Broadening a BJJ student's arsenal whilst respecting the legacy of jujutsu.

Focus on Positional Awareness
In BJJ, positional control and domination are highly valued. This is not by accident. It closely resembles the fundamentals of Judo and Jujutsu, which are kuzushi (off-balancing) and kumiuchi (grappling). The skill of throwing your opponent off balance and making space for throws or takedowns is known as kuzushi. This translates to BJJ as taking control of the battle by creating dominating positions like mount or back control that undermine your opponent's stability.

Similar to this, kumiuchi concentrates on grappling techniques to throw an opponent off-balance and then control and overpower them. This is a great fit with BJJ's emphasis on ground fighting and positioning opponents for submissions or sweeps.

Scenario-Based Training
Scenario-based training has deep origins in traditional martial arts such as Jujutsu, however, it is not limited to them. Integrating weapon defences, multiple assailants, and environmental conditions in these scenarios compelled students to modify their tactics and cultivate a more innate comprehension of self-defence.

For contemporary BJJ practitioners, this scenario-based training tradition offers several advantages – they can close the gap between application and technique by simulating the confusion and unpredictability of a genuine battle, scenario training enables BJJ practitioners to put their skills to the test in stressful situations.

BJJ practitioners gain confidence and resilience when they can effectively navigate difficult situations during training. They gain confidence in their abilities and learn how to solve problems under duress—qualities that are essential in a real-world self-defence situation.

BJJ practitioners respect the heritage of earlier martial arts while also getting ready for the unpredictability of self-defence scenarios by implementing scenario-based training. It's evidence of the ongoing worth and applicability of these conventional training techniques in the contemporary BJJ environment.

Brazilian Jiu Jitsu has undergone a remarkable journey from its humble beginnings in Japan to its current status as a global martial arts phenomenon. While its increasing popularity and focus on sport competition have raised concerns about a potential loss of effectiveness in real-world self-defence situations, BJJ practitioners can maintain the art's relevance and efficacy by returning to its roots and incorporating techniques and principles from traditional Japanese martial arts like Jujutsu.

By embracing the wisdom of the past and integrating it with modern training methods, such as scenario-based drills and a balanced approach to gi and no-gi training, Brazilian Jiu Jitsu can continue to evolve and thrive as a powerful, adaptive, and comprehensive system for self-defence and personal growth.

As practitioners and instructors, it is our responsibility to honour the rich heritage of Brazilian Jiu Jitsu while continually refining and expanding its capabilities to meet the challenges of an ever-changing world. By doing so, we ensure that the art remains true to its core values and maintains its position as a premier martial art for generations to come.

"I've always found that anything worth achieving will always have obstacles in the way and you've got to have that drive and determination to overcome those obstacles on route to whatever it is that you want to accomplish."
CHUCK NORRIS

Finding the Motivation to Train When Life Gets in the Way
by Sheryl Sumugat

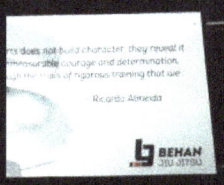  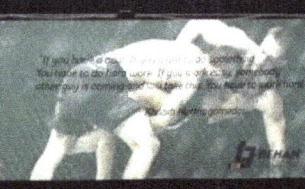

Behan Jiu Jitsu Gym, Toowoomba, QLD

Image by: Sheryl Sumugat

Finding motivation to train gets harder when life gets in the way. There have been a few times when I just wanted to go anywhere else but the gym.

One evening, I was already dressed up in my Gi when my two little girls started crying. Against my advice, my husband peeled the orange for them. They did not like that. In fact, they hated it so much they were inconsolable. They much prefer the way I do it: small slices with the skin on. All hell broke loose just when I was about to finally escape. I was upset with my husband and annoyed with my kids. It had been a long day.

As I stepped onto the carpeted floor of our gym, I wanted to burst into tears. *Why do I keep coming here where I just feel like a complete failure?* Jiu Jitsu is an ego-crushing sport where you literally end up on the bottom while someone heavy and sweating towers over you. *What the hell am I doing here?* I thought to myself. Life is already doing a good job submitting me and making me feel like a total noob. Am I a masochist?

I rarely feel excited to train these days when I'm tired and sleep deprived. I kind of wished I had started Jiujitsu before I became a mum. I am obsessed with this art, but I have bigger priorities and even bigger responsibilities. I show up and roll with people bigger and stronger than me who have the luxury of training every day and sleep for 8 hours. I am practically a sandbag even to people who have just started. I can't remember the moves I've just learned two weeks ago, my cardio is bad, and my mind is somewhere else. It's hard to switch off mothering so I can start smothering. Even when I'm on the mat, I worry about home. It's almost impossible to be mentally present when you've left the house in disarray.

But the great thing about going to the gym is you also meet people who feel the same way. There are at least five other mums like me in our gym who show up whenever they can, sometimes with their babies and kids. It's hard to make excuses when you have someone like Makayla who competed just months after giving birth to her third child. I would see Amber coming in with her baby girl in one arm and her gym bag in the other. She would wait for her partner to arrive so she could jump in and train. Brit still finds time to train even after her maternal leave. We have Emma who has transitioned from the women only class to the regular class, putting in more hours to her training. And Christianne has just become the first female brown belt in our gym.

My gym mates who aren't parents have their own struggles too. They are different for a variety of folks. Being a part of this gym community enables me to see past my own derelictions and think out of my own bubble. These struggles may be physical or mental health conditions, financial constraints, relationship troubles, waning interest, and whatnot. We all face some hardships, one way or another. And yet, here we are, sweating on the mat, doing a sport that doesn't look fun to most outsiders.

We are getting demolished by our training partners, sometimes you get a knee on your belly. If you get lucky you might get a knee on your face.

So why do it? you may ask. I do it because it teaches me to be patient. When you're in the losing position or even when you're winning, acting on impulse will be your downfall. Jiu Jitsu has revealed so many things about me, like my tendency to spaz or freeze, depending on the circumstance. Time on the mat has taught me to relax even when my training partner is mounted on me. Even though I still get submitted often, I get frustrated less because I've learned how to accept defeat. And in accepting defeat, I get to learn from my mistakes and do better in the next round. It used to upset me when I couldn't remember how to do a submission right or when I couldn't control my training partner. Well, it still does. But I've had a better understanding of what my bigger goal is, and that is to be anti-fragile. Anti-fragility is the ability to keep a positive disposition and a winning mindset despite being in the bottom position, to keep trying until it's over. The fact that any of us still show up—albeit begrudgingly at times—is already a win.

Of course, there's also the self-defence aspect. I train in Jiujitsu because I want to be prepared when God forbid, I am being attacked. This sport turns it into a game. Positional sparring forces you to be on the defensive, in a position you'd do your hardest not to end up in. You laugh, you curse under your breath, but there's no real harm because you're in a controlled environment. Eventually, you get used to it. Eventually, you perfect a sweep or a submission. If you face a rapist or an attacker, it would be unrealistic to say you'd easily annihilate them, like in one of those superhero films. You'd probably still get hurt, but you'd stand a better chance at surviving than if you haven't trained at all. Sure, it's going to be scary as hell but the longer you've trained, the better your body would be able to handle this stress response. You already know what to look out for, what not to do, and how to punish your attacker without the need for a weapon. YOU are the weapon.

As I'm writing this, I think fondly of my training partners, including the rough ones and the 'ego-checkers'. I think of brown belt Jason and Curtis who are always happy to roll with white belts and give them feedback and tips. There are a few higher belts at our gym who would adjust their skills and strength for their female rolling partners, especially ones like me who are small and barely surviving.

They let you taste a little bit of victory. They build you up to keep you motivated and interested. But the rough ones are also important. They make you feel like a rag-doll, but if you have the right mindset and attitude, this experience will only make you hungrier for growth and intensity. They remind you how it really is in the real world, and we all need reminding of that too sometimes.

I know I will have moments of weakness again where I'll feel like quitting and doing Zumba instead. But I also know that I'm not alone in this. Sometimes a PEP talk won't be enough; we'll be needing some encouragement from our training partners and coaches.

That is the importance of finding a good gym and seeking out people who are struggling like you but who keep on showing up for the love of the sport. But most importantly, resist the urge to compare yourself with others. Some people have been doing contact sports since they were three, and some are just blessed with a lot of time for training. Be happy for them and count your blessings. I'm not gonna lie; it sucks being with a training partner who's had better sleep, and sometimes you'll be tempted to throw in the towel and come back when life is a little bit easier.

The trouble is, you might never wanna come back and life might never give you that break you think you need. In that case, we must remember that there's more to life than Jiujitsu, and there's more to Jiujitsu than belts, medals, or submitting an opponent. Is this struggle worth it? I say, a struggle is worth it if even in defeat, we get something out of it.

Jiujitsu is definitely worth it.

Helping Others in the Dojo
BY CHRIS MCVAY

Hi guys, Aikido Chris here. Here are a few things I have been learning whilst training in the past few months.

When training with absolute beginners, it's hard for them to attack like they would without the experience of knowledgeable students. There are a few ways I've learnt so far to help them figure this out and how to relax.

Certain moves in Aikido and many other arts require a way in which to hold your hands out into the air or move in a circle to make the move more effective. One philosophy I came up with a fun one to remember. The move is called Sayu. This is basically swinging your arms from left to right. One hand is at your gut area and the other is up in the air on the other side.

I call this the 'air guitar swing'. When a beginner try's this move during an attack or defence, their palms are often in the other way or just not in the best way for them. My fun way of explaining this is, when you have a bubble bath and you pick up the bubbles to blow them away, you will have a flat hand. With the hand in that position, you can achieve a way to lead the other person where they need to go. There are other ways to explain this, but this is one I remember well.

How to help others with certain distraction techniques. Sometimes, when an opponent is going to strike, you must see certain parts of them move before you know it's on its way. These all happen in a split second. I call that the poker face. You can often tell when someone is focused on a strike and when they are going to do it by the funny faces they pull. Just as they strike if you're not quick enough but see their face. You can say something. Usually 'squirrel' comes to mind. It often gets a laugh.

You can find Chris at Port Kennedy Aikido www.AikidoPortKennedy.com

Aikido is a straightforward martial art which is based on defence and using the opponent's energy against them. Many people think martial arts are aggressive, hurt, and you must be young. This is not the case with Aikido. The main thing that martial arts work on is your own self. How much you put in is how much you gain. It is not a race, and it's not to see who is best. We all like that as people, but in the end, each class is a great experience and you gain great friends and an extended family.

I have also seen many people who have come to class who seem to be down or a little sad. Even if you're unhappy at the beginning of class, you nearly always go home at the end of the night with a great feeling of accomplishment and feel happy with yourself like all the worries of the world left you alone for the hour and a half class you had. It's truly amazing what a good class can give a person and how much you can learn even if you don't do any of the hard stuff there's always a fun person there that is more than willing to take the extra time and leave no one behind.

KARATE SELF-ESTEEM EGO & THE ID

by Tim Nicklin

Can we truly get rid of our ego without getting rid of our self-esteem? If not, then why do so many martial art teachers demand that we do, and why should we do such a thing? Do they know why or is it just a cliche, something just to say? One thing is certain in life, all the high achievers have egos and sometimes big egos and that's also true of martial art competition champions. They may be polite, they may be humble, but something drove them to win, and that something was self-belief (the self is the Id and the ego speaks for the Id) so why shut it down? Why get rid of it? It makes no sense in the modern western world, as however humble you see yourself, if you are seeing yourself; that's your ego.

In this piece I intend to look at two psychological points of view, the first from Sigmund Freud (1923) and his work on the Id (self) and then add some of my own opinions from my own training experience over many years and many countries.

Freud has the view that we have a split ego, part of which we are born with and part of which grows up with us (or in some cases this may not occur). The first part, the part we are born with I shall refer to as the infantile ego and the second part is the part that grows with us, I shall refer to as the ideal ego. Although Freud himself refers to this ego as the superego, however that leads to too much misunderstanding, as many people take that to mean inflated ego which it is not. If anything, the infantile ego is the inflated ego and the one we need to bring under control, and that's where most martial art teachers go so wrong, they try to suppress your ideal ego when it's this portion of the ego, according to Freud that we need to suppress or educate the infantile ego(self).

According to Freud, we are born with the infantile ego, it knows only as our internal environment. So, I want feeding; I scream, I want changing; I scream, I want attention ad infinitum et cetera.

I scream and scream and cry and cry until I get what I want just like a telephone in the corner that will not stop ringing until you answer it. This ego is totally solipsistic and narcissistic in its nature, it may be the "rider riding the horse" as Freud says, but it can't tell the horse where to go if it has not enough willpower of thought to change the horse's course.

This is where the ideal ego comes into play, as we grow this second half of our ego it grows with us helping us deal with the outside world teaching us manners, patience, social, interaction ad infinitum et cetera it's this ideal ego sometimes called the superego that we need. It will have hereditary traits, but it will also be individual to us. It is this ego that has confused some martial art teachers and many others in sport or business. When the teacher, sports coach or boss tells us to drop our ego they are doing so to control our thoughts and reactions toward external situations we will encounter in real life. Without this ideal portion of our ego we are left only with the infantile ego and we all know a solipsist narcissistic person or two, don't we? These are people who never actually got control of their mature ideal ego and therefore react to external situations with the infantile ego, meaning they act as a young child having no understanding of how to interact toward others, this leads to them demanding special treatment from others in the same way a baby or young child screams for its mother. For some reason or other, they never had to start the problem-solving process as they interacted with people in social situations.

The ideal ego is somewhat like a pilot guiding us where we need to go when interacting with others, so in martial arts where we constantly interact with others at very close proximity, the ideal ego is very much needed to overcome the selfish nature of the infantile ego. We must learn that we all have a valid place within the dojo and that all are there to learn and allow others to learn.

These skills of interaction are essential to kumite (partner work, on combat sport or self-defense) and Oyo no kata (practical use of kata, application of kata), as when practicing such subjects, it would be totally unacceptable to actually start to really break arms, legs or cracking skulls open. We may suffer the odd black eye or bruised ribs, but for the most part in dojo practice, we understand that we are not in actual combat but practicing an art. So, we endeavor to respect each other by treating others how we ourselves would wish to be treated.

The Golden rule of the Roman Emperor Alexander Severus AD 209-235 was Quod tibi fieri non vis alteri ne feceris (what you do not wish done to yourself, do not do to others) So these ideas on using your self-esteem (how you see yourself in self-respect { the ideal ego}) being used to judge how we should treat others are not new to the western world and it would be very hard to remove from our psyche, leaving us incapable of interacting with each other in the dojo unless constantly under direct control of a teacher, leaving absolutely no room for self-discovery or self-awareness of our martial techniques or strategies making advancement impossible.

So, reflecting upon this, I would say ego (self) is as important to martial arts as it is to life itself and this also fits precisely with the first principle of Grand Master Gichen Funakoshi of Shotokan fame. Funakoshi's first principle of karate is - karate Do wa rei ni hajimari, rei ni owaru koto O wasureru na (do not forget that karate begins and ends with respect). Funakoshi himself explains this in his book on his twenty principles. Rei is often defined as" respect "but it means much more. Rei encompasses both an attitude of respect for others and a sense of self-esteem. When those who honour themselves transfer that feeling of esteem, and respect to others, their action is nothing less than an expression of rei.

So, we can see from a western point of view following Sigmund Freud's work and mixing in some ancient ideas from Rome as well as a point from Okinawa in Funakoshi's first principle, the ego or self-esteem is important to karate.

However, this extends beyond karate. It teaches us that in life we need the ideal ego to teach us how to mix successfully with other people in all sorts of different and sometimes difficult situations. The ideal ego must be allowed to operate as a free agent in the dojo otherwise we will not learn ourselves how to operate as a free agent in life at work, at school, at university whether in a position of authority or as a student or employee, if our ideal ego is nurtured correctly in the dojo it will help us tremendously in life.

Dojo kumite is a perfect tool for nurturing the ego in this way as here we have no choice but to take note of our opponents. We must respect them as we would wish ourselves to be respected. Striking someone in an unfair manner whilst sparring (which is not fighting, as sparring is there to learn from not to win.) is unacceptable. When sparring in the Dojo with juniors or novice grades it's the senior's responsibility to make sure the sparring stays safe and educational, whilst still invoking an attitude of seriousness to teach the junior or novice the dangers of taking this exercise too flippantly.

These newly acquired skills developed in your heightened ideal ego should then be taken back to your kata, where you can then reflect upon them. In a meditational manner, trying your best to perfect the technique of understanding others and therefore giving you the advantage in any awkward real-life situations that you may find yourself in.

Having trained since childhood and having had the chance to train with some great people in some interesting countries and now in my 60th year, I feel I've had long enough time to ponder this question of ego. I honestly feel that karate, kata, and kumite are the perfect training exercises to help us better understand our egos rather than removing them, therefore removing ourselves from ourselves.

Tim Nicklin
7th Dan Niwa Dojo,
Western Australia.

References
Freud, S. (1923). The Ego and the Id. London: Hogarth Press.
Funakoshi, G. (1938). The Twenty Guiding Principles of Karate. London: Kodansha International Ltd.

POWERFUL FUSION YOGA & MARTIAL ARTS

By Leanne Canning
www.womenawaredefence.com

Image by Mikhail Nilov

If you're a martial artist seeking to diversify your training regimen, yoga is an amazing addition that can bring remarkable benefits. It's a unique blend of flexibility, strength, and balance, mindfulness and breath control. These are all crucial elements to reach your full potential in martial arts. In this article I will show you how yoga and martial arts intertwine and delve into some of the best yoga poses that you can add to your training routine. As both a martial artist and yoga practitioner the sky is the limit when you combine the two.

YOGA AND MARTIAL ARTS COMPLIMENT EACH OTHER

For many people they appear to be so different from each other. Martial arts is all about fighting techniques and self-defense. Yoga emphasises on calmness, flexibility, and inner peace. But they both share a common core, deeply rooted in physical and mental discipline, balance, breath control, and focus. The powerful fusion yoga & martial arts provides a spiritual approach to fitness that combines the kinetic dynamism of martial arts with the tranquility and balance that yoga processes.

Yoga's spiritual benefits are well-documented: enhanced flexibility, improving balance, building your core strength, body awareness, stress reduction, and enhancing your focus. These elements also directly contribute to martial arts performance by promoting fluidity in movements, improving balance and stability, reducing the risk of injuries, and honing mental acuity. Thus, integrating yoga into your martial arts training can significantly elevate your physical prowess and mental resilience.

7 REASONS WHY YOGA IS BENEFICIAL IN MARTIAL ARTS

1. FLEXIBILITY
I am sure everybody has heard how yoga is amazing and gives you flexibility you could only dream of. Yes, it's true. Think about it a whole class designed to bending, twisting, arching, and inverting your body to its fullest.

No, being flexible is not a prerequisite to joining yoga. Very few people walk in the first day already able to hold all the poses perfectly. And where would the fun be in the journey? Just like martial arts training , the more you train the better the results.

2. BREATHING TECHNIQUES
Regardless if you are a runner, martial artist or boxer. In order to work at optimal athletic performance you need to have a good breathing technique. For proper pacing, decision-making under stress, and recovery between rounds: huffing and puffing through your mouth is not optimal. Many yoga practices encourage you to maintain nasal-diaphragm breathing for the entire duration of the class. And you can take this directly into your training. I can't count the number of times I've been astounded by the levels of mouth breathing on the mats. Do yoga; don't be a mouth-breather.

3. BALANCE
Holding various yoga poses leads to better awareness of your body parts in space (kinaesthetic intelligence) leads to improved balance and movement.
 If you're wobbly on your feet, this is for you. Stand-up martial arts can especially benefit from balance training. General stability is important for both young and old, but balance poses can also be very useful for older athletes and fall prevention.

4. STRENGTH
Thinking that yoga class is equal to nap time is a common misconception. Although it's generally light-intensity, there is a lot of bodyweight strength involved - core, legs, shoulders - you name it. For all the gains, aim to hold a pose for 5 deep breaths rather than hopping quickly from one Asana to the next. Having to keep yourself in a position for a longer time builds strength, as opposed to the use of pure momentum to get you in and out of a posture. For example, a slow descent from the plank position to the ground (Chatturanga Dandasana) is basically an eccentric push-up, building upper-body strength.

5. FOCUS
Controlling your breath throughout the entire practice, and focusing your gaze on a single fixed point (Drishti) are two key ways that yoga turns your senses inward to a highly-focused state of mind. Your ability to maintain concentration for an extended period of time is known as Dharana, which is one step before entering meditation. It should be easy to imagine how this mental fortitude would be a valuable skill to have during sparring rounds, pad-work training, and even conditioning. All will require that you overcome both mental and physical hurdles.

6. BODY AWARENESS
Get to know your own anatomy. Physically, you'll soon find out where your muscular imbalances are, and what anatomical advantages and disadvantages you have. Some things like hamstring flexibility can be improved, but other aspects like hip rotation often need to be adapted to. No two bodies are the same, just as no two fighters are the same. You're not expected to imitate the yoga teacher exactly; you're expected to find the version of the pose that fits your body. For example, a 6-foot-tall BJJ athlete doesn't normally have the same game-plan as a 5-foot BJJ athlete. Learn about your anatomy and take it into your training.

7. SELF REFLECTION
Blessed are those with the ability to look at themselves objectively - and yoga is a great tool for developing this. Sitting with yourself at the end of trainingin a relaxed state, breath regulated, Parasympathetic Nervous System (PNS) activated: your mind is an empty sheet, primed for soft focus and calm contemplation on your thoughts and emotions. There is so much ego in martial arts. (If you're unaware of this, you may be part of the problem.) Introspection is a key element in yoga that can help to tame that wild ego. Avoid the temptation to skip the Pranayama (breathing practice) or Savasana at the end of a training session. Contrary to popular belief, moments of stillness can bring you as much of the long-term benefits all the stretchy, flashy poses can, and then some.

In short - yoga is like a hidden secret that some people have unlocked, and others have dismissed before they've even tried. Like your new favourite song, it can take a few tries before it catches on. Give yoga a chance!

Now, let's delve into some specific yoga poses that can complement and enhance your martial arts practice. Each pose will be accompanied by a brief description of its benefits and the martial arts aspects it complements.

DOWNWARD-FACING DOG

A staple in many yoga practices, this pose is a forward bend and mild inversion that stretches the entire body. It increases flexibility in the hamstrings and calves, strengthens the arms and shoulders, and improves circulation to the brain.

How it aids Martial Arts: Greater arm and shoulder strength can enhance striking power. Improved lower body flexibility aids in executing high kicks and dodging attacks. Increased blood flow to the brain can promote quicker decision-making in sparring situations.

WARRIOR 2 POSE

This pose strengthens the legs, opens the hips and chest, and cultivates focus. It encourages full body awareness, as you're required to maintain a strong lower body stance while opening the torso and gazing forward.

How it aids Martial Arts: Stronger legs and open hips can enhance stance stability and kicking ability. The open chest fosters a relaxed, ready position, and the forward gaze is akin to the focus required in martial arts.

TREE POSE

Tree Pose improves balance, strengthens the ankles and calves, and enhances concentration and focus. As a single-leg balancing pose, it can also help cultivate patience and mindfulness.

How it aids Martial Arts: Better balance directly translates to more effective movement in martial arts, from maintaining a strong stance to executing controlled kicks. Greater ankle strength can help prevent injuries during rapid direction changes common in martial arts.

BRIDGE POSE

This backbend pose strengthens the back and opens the chest and shoulders. It can also stimulate the abdominal organs, improving digestion.

How it aids Martial Arts: A strong back can contribute to better posture and reduce the risk of injury during falls or throws. Open chest and shoulders can improve breathing, which is essential for endurance during prolonged bouts.

SEATED FORWARD BEND

This calming pose stretches the spine, shoulders, and hamstrings. It also stimulates the internal organs and can improve digestion.

How it aids Martial Arts: Greater spine flexibility can improve agility and reduce the risk of back injuries. Improved hamstring flexibility can enable higher and more fluid kicks.

BOAT POSE

This core-strengthening pose challenges your balance while engaging your abdominals. It can also stimulate the kidneys, thyroid, and intestines.

How it aids Martial Arts: A strong core can improve overall strength and stability, which is essential for powerful strikes, throws, and maintaining control during grapples.

TRIANGLE POSE

This pose stretches the hips, groins, and hamstrings, opens the chest and shoulders, and improves balance. It can also stimulate the abdominal organs and aid digestion.

How it aids Martial Arts: The flexibility gained in the hips and hamstrings can enhance the range of motion in kicks and stances. Improved balance and a more open chest can contribute to better performance and endurance.

PLANK POSE

The plank pose is a powerful core strengthener that also works the arms, wrists, and legs. It improves posture and can help prevent back pain.

How it aids Martial Arts: Stronger core and arm muscles can improve power in punches and stability during grappling. A stronger back can help prevent injuries from falls and enhance posture for efficient movement. Showing the powerful fusion yoga & martial arts.

CROW POSE

This advanced pose develops arm and wrist strength, core power, and balance. It's also an excellent pose for developing mental focus and body awareness.

How it aids Martial Arts: Strength gained in the wrists and arms can enhance grappling and blocking skills. Improved balance and body awareness can contribute to better control and precision in techniques.

PIGEON POSE

29

Pigeon Pose is a deep hip opener that also stretches the thighs, glutes, and psoas. It promotes flexibility and releases tension.

How it aids Martial Arts: The flexibility gained can contribute to a higher range of motion in kicks and stances. Releasing tension in these areas can also reduce the risk of strains and sprains.

CORPSE POSE

This restorative pose may look easy, but it's all about relaxation and stress relief. It trains the body and mind to achieve a deep state of rest, aiding recovery and promoting a mindful, balanced state.

How it aids Martial Arts: Enhanced recovery can speed up muscle healing after strenuous training. The mindfulness and relaxation skills learned can help manage stress and maintain calm during bouts.

PRANAYAMA

Let's not forget one of the most vital aspects of yoga: pranayama or breath control. Pranayama exercises can help improve lung capacity, focus, and stress control—all beneficial for martial arts. For instance, Ujjayi breathing, also known as "Victorious Breath," can help maintain rhythm in your movements and keep you calm and centred even in high-stress sparring situations.

Remember, each person's body is different. Always pay attention to your body's signals and respect your limits. It's important to maintain a consistent yoga practice for sustained benefits, but overdoing it can lead to injuries.

Also, consider seeking guidance from a qualified yoga instructor, especially when starting. They can help ensure correct alignment and provide modifications for different fitness levels or restrictions. A class environment can also offer a family feeling and support as you explore the integration of yoga and martial arts.

Incorporating yoga into your martial arts routine is a journey of self-discovery, health, and improved performance. Enjoy this holistic approach to training, and experience the enhanced mental clarity, physical strength, and inner peace that this fusion offers.

THE PHILOSOPHY CONNECTION

While yoga and martial arts share many physical similarities, their philosophical underpinnings also intersect. Both disciplines preach respect—respect for the self, for others, and for the practice. This mutual respect fosters a healthy training environment, deepens personal growth, and builds strong community bonds.

Also, martial arts and yoga both stress the importance of being in the moment. Whether you're executing a difficult pose or defending against an opponent, the ability to focus entirely on the present is paramount. Practicing mindfulness can enhance the execution of techniques, improve reaction times, and reduce the likelihood of injuries.

By adding the powerful fusion yoga & martial arts together offers more than just physical benefits. It cultivates mental fortitude, presence, and focus, underscoring the unity of mind and body that is fundamental to both arts. Regardless if you're a blackbelt martial artist or a beginner, introducing yoga into your training can contribute to an elevated, spiritual approach to your practice. Experience this symbiotic relationship and allow it to guide your journey in the martial arts realm.

As I love training in both, when I restarted my martial arts journey, I discovered by incorporating yoga into my routine. It greatly enhanced not only my physical martial arts skills, but also gave me clarity mentally. Even the younger practitioners in karate, would ask about how I was so flexible. I would also say that I practiced yoga. Remember, it's essential to approach both disciplines with respect and patience. Listen to your body, pace yourself, and keep your intentions clear as you embark on this enriching path.

Quinoa, Avocado, and Grilled Chicken Salad

Quinoa, Avocado, and Grilled Chicken Salad

For a healthy and easy-to-prepare post-training meal:

Ingredients:

- 1 cup quinoa, rinsed
- 2 cups water
- 2 boneless, skinless chicken breasts
- 1 ripe avocado, diced.
- 1 cucumber, diced
- 1 red capsicum, diced
- 1/4 cup crumbled feta cheese
- 2 tbsp olive oil
- 1 lemon, juiced
- Salt and pepper to taste
- Fresh herbs (like parsley or coriander) for

Instructions:

- Cook quinoa according to package instructions (typically, bring 2 cups of water to a boil, add 1 cup of rinsed quinoa, reduce heat to low, cover, and simmer for 15-20 minutes until water is absorbed).

- While the quinoa is cooking, season chicken breasts with salt and pepper. Grill or pan-fry the chicken until cooked through and golden brown. Let it rest for a few minutes, then slice into strips.

- In a large bowl, combine cooked quinoa, diced avocado, cucumber, red capsicum, and crumbled feta cheese.

- In a small bowl, whisk together olive oil, lemon juice, salt, and pepper to create a dressing.

- Pour the dressing over the quinoa salad and toss to combine.

- Top the salad with sliced grilled chicken and garnish with fresh herbs.

This meal is packed with protein from the chicken and quinoa, healthy fats from the avocado and olive oil, and fibre and vitamins from the vegetables. The lemon juice and feta add a bright, tangy flavour to the dish. You can easily customise this salad by adding or substituting your favourite vegetables or toppings.

Remember to stay hydrated and listen to your body's needs after training. Enjoying a nutritious and satisfying meal like this one can support your recovery and help you feel your best for your next training session.

Healthy Nut Slice

Ingredients:
- 1 cup almonds
- 1 cup walnuts
- 1 cup pitted dates
- 1/2 cup dried cranberries
- 1/2 cup unsweetened shredded coconut
- 1/4 cup chia seeds
- 1/4 cup pumpkin seeds
- 1/4 cup sunflower seeds
- 2 tbsp coconut oil
- 1 tsp vanilla extract
- 1/2 tsp cinnamon
- Pinch of salt

Instructions:

- Line a 20x20 cm baking dish with baking paper, allowing the paper to overhang on the sides for easy removal.

- In a food processor, pulse the almonds and walnuts until they are finely chopped but not turning into a paste.

- Add the pitted dates, dried cranberries, shredded coconut, chia seeds, pumpkin seeds, and sunflower seeds to the food processor. Pulse until the mixture is well combined and sticks together.

- In a small microwave-safe bowl, melt the coconut oil. Add the melted coconut oil, vanilla extract, cinnamon, and salt to the food processor. Pulse until everything is well combined, and the mixture holds together when pressed.

- Transfer the mixture to the prepared baking dish and press it down firmly and evenly using a spatula or your hands.

- Place the baking dish in the refrigerator for at least 1 hour to allow the slice to set.

- Once set, remove the slice from the baking dish using the overhanging baking paper. Cut into squares or bars.

- Store the slices in an airtight container in the refrigerator for up to a week, or in the freezer for up to a month.

This nut-based vegetarian slice is packed with healthy fats, fibre, and protein from the various nuts and seeds. The dates and dried cranberries provide natural sweetness, while the coconut oil, vanilla, and cinnamon add depth of flavour. It's a perfect snack to fuel your body before or after a workout, or to enjoy as a healthy treat any time of day.

"We have more faith in what we imitate than in what we originate. We cannot derive a sense of absolute certitude from anything which has its root in us. The most poignant sense of insecurity comes from standing alone; we are not alone when we imitate."

Bruce Lee

The French Disconnection

by Attila Halasz

Having shared my Austrian Aikido adventure in the previous issue, it is time to reveal what happened at this two day international Aikido seminar during the summer of 1995.

The French fourth dan was cool upon arrival, wearing sunglasses out on the football field where nearly eighty participants gathered. A really mixed crowd with a few black belts from Central Europe. As expected, all conformed to the French instructor's current, Japanese hombu dojo style of Aikido.

Not me, however.

Master Ken in my home dojo Paddington, Australia emphasised working with ki energy, at all times as it was originally taught by grandmaster Koichi Tohei, the 10th dan chief instructor of the Japanese Hombu Dojo until 1974.

After that, however, ki Aikido was no longer welcome there.

Being a young Australian black belt in 1995 with no exposure to other dojos I thought ALL Aikido schools worked with ki.

The seminar gained momentum, all black belts lined up in front with a sea of white belts behind. The French teacher, as he walked around, often glanced at me from the corner of his eye. He knew most of the present European black belts, from previous camps. He certainly never met me.

I was first paired with a 2nd dan from the Czech Republic as we were working on some basic throws. I didn't understand, he was ranked higher than me so why doesn't he use his ki?

"Why the ghost shell?" I asked. He looked puzzled, so I threw him.
"That's interesting!" He responded. He added that he never trained with ki before.

The opening morning class was ending, and we finished with a seated technique called 'Kokyu Dosa' in my dojo but they called it 'Kokyu Ho' over there.

My white belt training partner held both my wrist strongly as I threw him light as air relying on the power of ki. I've done this exercise for years as instructed by master Ken. But this was the point when the French guy had enough of me and my ki.

He clapped his hands and called out loudly, "Stop!"

Everyone gathered around.

"This is a prime example of training incorrectly." He pointed at me, still sitting with the white belt.

"This type of fantasy that at shodan level a person is able to throw someone with ki is actually detrimental to true aikido. Your technique will simply not work in a real situation or against a strong, experienced opponent." He added.

To make an example out of me, he signalled to one of his large 3rd dans to come forward and perform the exercise with me. The selected Hungarian teacher grabbed my wrists like iron.

It did not bother me, as I have been training this technique with some real beasts at home. Since an example was needed, I closed my eyes and extended my ki even more with only the smallest of physical movements and threw the giant with ease on both sides.

The French instructor came closer.

"No, no...don't give him leeway, grab him properly!" He urged the giant.

This time the 3rd dan grabbed me with even more power but the results were just the same. "I grabbed him as strong as I could!" he finally said it to the French.

I turned to him also.
"Perhaps you want to experience the ways of ki yourself?"

The huge crowd watched on in total silence. There was a clear moment of incredible embarrassment for the French instructor.

"Right …let's move on. We continue with standing breathing exercises." With that, he turned his back on me and walked away.

In more ways than one.

During that afternoon and all the next day, he never looked at me or called me up for a demonstration or ukemi.

At meal breaks, he sat with his organisation's black belts. Naturally, I wasn't invited. I ended up sitting with the white belts in a different corner. Since I paid for the seminar, I decided to stick it out.

As I was clearly out of favour, the other black belts were careful not to pair with me.

On the other hand, and on a positive note, word spread that "The Australian black belt isn't rough with the joint locks", which this weekend intensive, much focused on.

Ki has gentle ways, and the white belts rushed at the chance to work with me.

On the last day, when the training camp came to a close and the instructor was whisked away to his hotel by his hosts (I stayed in a tent, with a white belt), something totally unexpected happened.

Since almost all of the black belts avoided me during the intensive I was quite shocked to see a few of them surrounding me now as I packed up my gear.

The 3rd dan, who couldn't stop me, spoke first.

"Man, that was incredible. I always wanted to train with somebody from the ki Aikido style. When in Budapest, please visit and teach a couple of classes in my dojo." He handed me a business card. I received a similar invite from an Austrian dojo and the 2nd dan from the Czech Republic. As I was leaving, many of the friendly white belts shook my hand.

This turned out to be a pretty good training camp after all.

A few weeks later I was in beautiful Budapest, took up the offer and taught a couple ki aikido classes.

Out at dinner, my host turned to me.

"If you are still around in a few months time, a prominent Japanese 8th dan, personal student of the founder, Morihei Ueshiba, will be in town for a 5 day seminar." He gave me the details.

What?!

Someone who was there? Someone who trained together with Koichi Tohei as well?

I was beside myself.
I am definitely going!

At best I was expecting some superior aikido. Had no idea that the encounter would change my life and thinking forever. But that's another story.

Koichi Tohei was a 10th Dan aikidoka and founder of the Ki Society and its style of aikido, officially Shin Shin Toitsu Aikido, but commonly known as Ki-Aikido.

PART I

Kobudo is the forgotten brother of karate. When karate changed from Tang/Chinese hand (唐手) to empty hand (空手), the art of weaponry originally practised by the old masters of karate started to slowly vanish. Kanga 'Tode' Sakugawa was famous for his bojutsu, his student Sōkon Matsumura, and later Matsumura's student Anko Azato, were noted masters of Jigen-ryu, a sword-fighting art brought to Okinawa by the Satsuma samurais.

The Motobu brothers, Choyu and Choki, both practised Jigen-ryu [10] while Chotoku Kyan practised bojutsu and taught it to all of his students. Even Gichin Funakoshi brought bojutsu with him when he first came to mainland Japan, something modern karateka seems to have conveniently forgotten. Perhaps the oldest reference we have of Kobudo being practised together with Karate is Chatan Yara, from the 17th century, who practised bo, sai, and eku (oar). Chatan Yara no Sai is still a kata performed in several styles to this day.

Kobudo means 'ancient martial art', which, let's be honest, is a very generic name that sheds no light whatsoever. In this context, what it refers to is the weaponry of Okinawa, the rokushaku bo (6-feet staff) being the most ubiquitous. The history of kobudo is very intricate and murky, similar to the history of prewar karate.

There are, however, some things about kobudo's history that we do know of. A prevailing myth is that kobudo was only practised by farmers using their farming tools after the Satsuma banned weapons in Okinawa. We know this to be false as most kobudo masters were nearly all part of the Yukatchu (aristocratic) and Aji (royalty) classes, Sanra Chinen perhaps being the sole exception [1], just like the karate masters. We can also see this in the prevalent use of metal weapons like the sai, tekko, and tinbe-rochin which would be too expensive for the Heimin (commoner) class.

The three main styles of kobudo are Matayoshi Kobudo, Yamane-ryu, and Ryukyu Kobudo. There are, of course, offshoots of these three styles as well as unique kobudo integrated into karate styles like in Isshin-ryu and Ryuei-ryu. Each of these styles have their own unique characteristics and history.

Ryukyu Kobudo is to kobudo what Shito-ryu is to karate. Taira Shinken created the style to preserve as much traditional Okinawan kobudo as he could accumulate, which means that this style has the highest number of kata [11]. The movements of Ryukyu Kobudo also look more standardised and refined, a bit more mainland-influenced. For this reason, it is perhaps the best portrayal of generic kobudo across the Ryukyu Islands.

Taira Shinken originally learned kobudo from Yabiku Moden [12]. Moden was a student of Ankō Itosu, but he seemed to have specialised in kobudo. Ryukyu Kobudo was first started to preserve Moden's kobudo, which was mostly based on old-style Yamane-ryu bojutsu, but along the way, Taira seemed to have collected far more kobudo than anyone.

Yamane-ryu (oki: Yamanni-ryu) traditionally only practised the bo, but has recently also incorporated other weapons into the style as well. Yamane-ryu was the kobudo of Chinen Sanra, also called Yamane Tanmei (Grandfather Yamane), Yamane Usume (Old Man Yamane), or Yamane Chinen (Chinen of Yamane), who was a peasant from, as you might have guessed, Yamane [1]. It is not clear where or whom Chinen learned his bojutsu, although one theory is that it came from Kanga Sakugawa. Another theory is that Chinen learned bojutsu from his village and innovated the rest himself. One way or another, Chinen achieved fame for his bojutsu that even the aristocrats learned from him. The style was succeeded by his grandson Masami Chinen.

The defining feature of the style is characterized by the extended grip along with very loose whipping cuts and bouncing of the bo. Unlike most other styles, Yamane-ryu has a focus on fluidity and relaxation. While anyone doing martial arts will be aware that muscling your technique is always bad, Yamane-ryu works in a way that muscling will actually render the technique useless, even to the point of injuring yourself.

Matayoshi Kobudo was kobudo as passed down through the Matayoshi family and finally culminating with Matayoshi Shinko and his son Matayoshi Shinpo. This style has perhaps the most weapons amongst all kobudo styles—albeit not the most kata, that honour belongs to Ryukyu Kobudo—, a lot being farming tools that were not actually made to be weapons such as the kuwa (hoe) and kama (sickle). The style's defining characteristics are the black dogi top and what I like to call 'T-rex hands' when gripping the bo. The T-rex hands gives us more flexibility and reach with our strikes, although it is admittedly quite unintuitive at the start and will require a certain degree of wrist mobility that needs some time to get used to. If anyone asks why we wear black dogi, the answer is because weapons that are regularly cleaned and oiled make white dogi dirty really fast. We will discuss more on Matayoshi Kobudo's history and curriculum in part two of this series.

A pattern, not rule, that I have observed personally is that Ryukyu Kobudo tends to be practised by mainland style practitioners, i.e. Shito-ryu and Shotokan, perhaps due to the close relationship between Taira with Funakoshi and Mabuni. Yamane-ryu tends to be practised by Shorin practitioners, be that of Chibana, Nagamine, or Kyan's lineages. Matayoshi Kobudo tends to be practised by Shorei/Naha-te practitioners.

Matayoshi Shinpo himself, Gakiya Yoshiaki, and Hidetada Ishiki all learned Goju-ryu while Takehiro Gaja, Josei Yogi, Shusei Maeshiro, and Takeshi Kinjo are all 9th-10th dan in Uechi-ryu. The background of these masters seem to have affected the way they each perform their kobudo.

If I were to compare the movements of each kobudo style with boxers, to give a hopefully more relatable picture, whereas Ryukyu Kobudo is the refined Vasyl Lomachenko and Yamane-ryu is the whipping Larry Holmes, Matayoshi Kobudo would be explosive Joe Louis.

References:
[1] Yamanni-ryu – Is the founder's name Sanrā, Sanda, Masanrā, or Saburō? | Ryukyu Bugei 琉球武芸
[2] https://kodokanboston.files.wordpress.com/2014/02/meibukanmagazine-no-9_matayoshi.pdf
[3] Shūshi no Kun (Bojutsu Kata Series) — History | Ryukyu Bugei 琉球武芸
[4] The lineage of Shushi nu kun | Thekaratepage.com
[5] The History and Contents of Matayoshi Kobudo as of 1999 | Ryukyu Bugei 琉球武芸
[6] Chōun no Kon (Morning Cloud's Staff) | by Motobu Naoki | Jan, 2024 | Medium
[7] Chōun no Kon – (Bojutsu Kata Series) | Ryukyu Bugei 琉球武芸
[8] Chōshi no Kon, Bō kata of Soeishi-ryū | by Motobu Naoki | Motobu-ryu Blog | Dec, 2023 | Medium
[9] Kingai-ryū Karate Okinawa Kobujutsu (Info translated from the Nihon Kobudō Kyōkai, 2022) | Ryukyu Bugei 琉球武芸
[10] Motobu Chōki's Wooden Sword. Written by Motobu Naoki, translated by... | by Motobu Naoki | Motobu-ryu Blog | Medium
[11] Kobudo kata list – then and now | Ryukyu Bugei 琉球武芸
[12] Taira Shinken – Restorer of Okinawa Kobudō | Ryukyu Bugei 琉球武芸

Bryan H. Wiratno from UWA Kobudo Club

Okinawan kobudo weapons including rokushaku bo staff, sai, tekko, tinbe-rochin shield and spear, kuwa hoe, kama sickle.

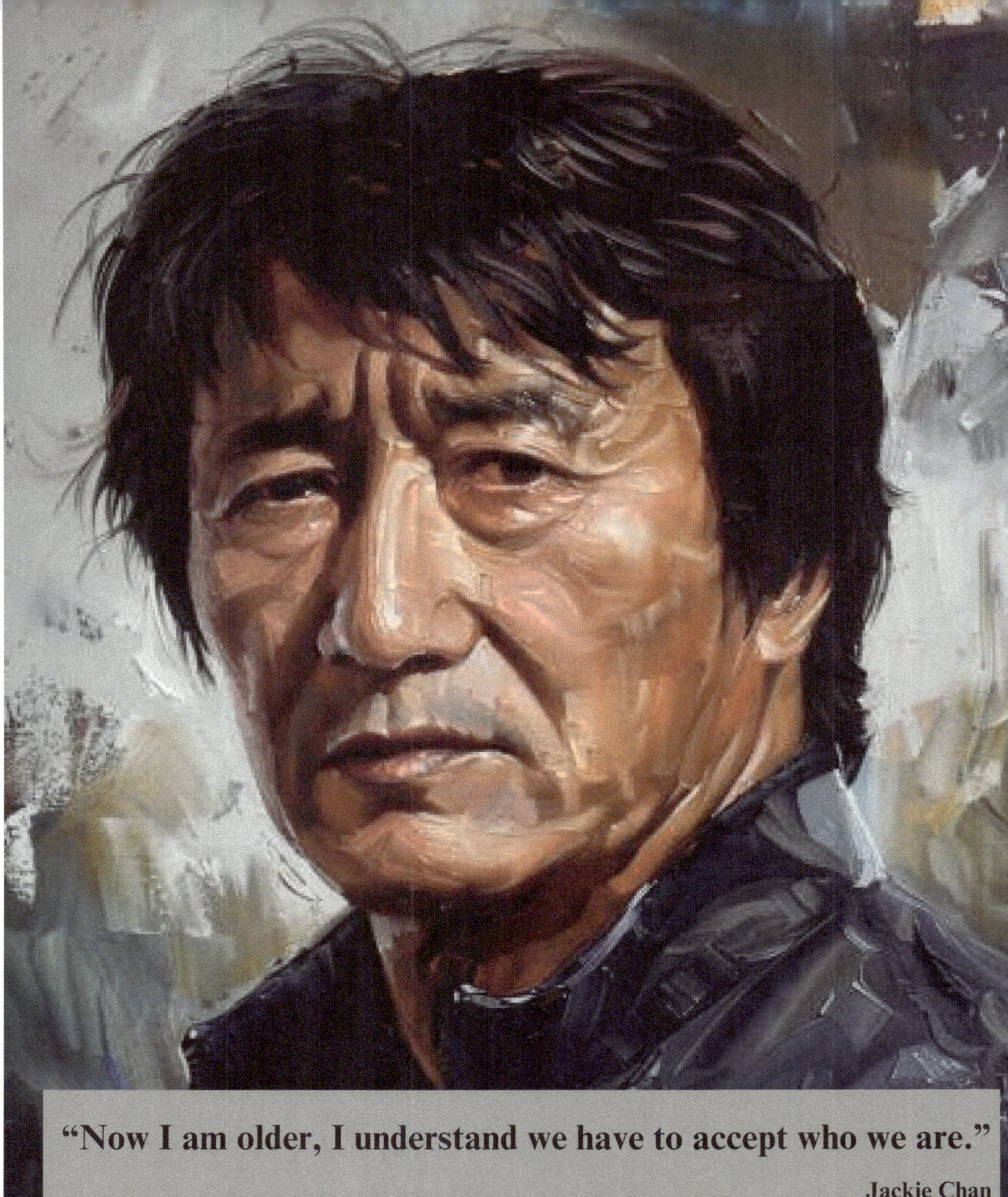

COMBAT ANALYSIS

'Jackie Chan vs The Jet in MEALS ON WHEELS'

by

Vance Ang

With news of an upcoming documentary on the life of kickboxing legend and martial arts pioneer, Benny 'The Jet' Urquidez (being spearheaded by none other than Keanu Reeves) it would be pertinent to look back over his fight career. And yet, through a more creative lens it is (at least in this writer's opinion) equally relevant to wax nostalgia and defer to his cinematic showings. There had been limited instances where he was cast as a hero, such as in FORCE FIVE (1981) alongside fellow martial arts alum such as Joe Lewis, Bong Soo Han and legendary Aussie, Richard Norton.Indeed, the fight scene between Richard Norton and Sammo Hung in TWINKLE TWINKLE LITTLE STARS (1985) deserves deconstruction but for another time.

His more memorable roles were certainly as a heel, or pro-wrestling speak as a villain. He was quietly imposing, menacing and never yielded to cookie cutter tropes of pure villainy – but as a bad guy, he rarely speaks but instead relies on pure ferocity in his characterisations. The irony, is that if you watch any of his interviews he speaks with enthusiasm, vibrance and a joyful quality that is very endearing. But if one watches him in either DRAGON's FOREVER (1988) or MEALS ON WHEELS (1986), the latter of which is the subject of this commentary, its true that he makes for an effective bad guy.

To some, this is the best fight scene ever committed to film and whilst it is dated in some aspects there is much to like and much to justify this claim.With mostly a wide shot utilised, devoid of that vomit inducing shaky-cam all the action is captured in full view of the audience with no cut aways and no doubles. To this day, the choreography is crisp, brutal and exciting to watch.

As with say an MMA fight, the opening seconds are dedicated to that 'combat market research' where the combatants are feeling out the opponent – gauging the early level of skill and assessing capabilities.

Decked out in a white suit, complete with suspenders Urquidez's bad guy is confident from the get go. He quickly discards the jacket with a swift spinning back kick to Chan, who rushes in and cops it sweet – the very move itself being a clear signature move of Urquidez in the ring, predating Cung Le's mastery of this move in the MMA cages by 20 years. The opening sections have The Jet dominating the fight, with his forward movement not only destabilising Chan's physical balance but also frightening him and putting him on the back foot. He becomes desperate and wild in his responses, with The Jet essentially managing the pacing and inviting his opponent to make errors. There is this pressurising flurry of punches that Urquidez launches against Chan with violent intent, and so powerful that it pushes Chan back into the dining table that itself retreats. Whilst the hero is literally on the back foot, Urquidez launches a spinning kick that actually blows out a set of candles – this was 1986 and this was no CGI, this was pure speed, precision and skill, courtesy of The Jet.

Eating more of the Jet's brutal kicks and punches, Chan's character becomes desperate, and this recklessness causes him to seize a chair in a counter move but one that his skilled opponent easily avoids. Perhaps to realise some respite, Chan still on the defensive opts for some grappling which The Jet easily counters and takes the fight back to one of the four ranges of combat, where he excels enabling him to punish his desperate opponent with more kicks and punches.

Interestingly, this not a David vs Goliath fight with both men equally matched in size but differing in skill. Therefore, as the hero Chan's character isn't forced to find a weakness in the same way Bruce Lee does against Kareem Abdul Jabbar in GAME OF DEATH (1978); but rather freely adapt to the scenario to calm himself and treat the bout like one of his usual training sessions which was foreshadowed in the opening scenes of the film. Easing back onto the floor, seemingly hiding behind a piece of furniture Chan locks eyes with his stronger and more skilled opponent – seeing the psychotic rage in the champion's eyes. The realisation that he cannot match The Jet in power and aggression, means that Chan decides to calm himself and become more fluid – and rather than rush in blindly, to take a moment, to breath, to assess and to think more critically about what he needs to do. Parking himself on a chair, seemingly even confuses Urquidez's character who looks confused and perplexed. Chan postures to see how Urquidez reacts, loosens himself and subtly invites Urquidez to attack which he does. This is what exceptional counter strikers like Conor McGregor is known for, to bait and to react but essentially ask your opponent what YOU want them to do.

It's at this moment that Urquidez opts to charge in, just as Chan did earlier and is met with quick reaction; he becomes more rigid and telegraphed whilst Chan's character is fluid and reactive, landing a spinning kick of his own that strikes The Jet across the temple. The fight psychology changes, and now he is in control of the tempo and pacing, treating the fight as not 'life or death' but rather an exercise routine enabling him to be calm and calculated. Indeed, he still eats strikes from his highly skilled opponent but these become inconsequential in the scheme of things. With the fight going against him, the once dominant Urquidez resorts to grappling which Chan cheekily answers with literal tickling to escape a lethal grip. Evidently, it can be viewed as a war of attrition with the hero out-performing the villain – but that in itself would be too simplistic. By removing the worry, the emotion and the fear the hero can victor by taking a moment to stop and relax; even in the heat of the moment in a pressurised scenario, decreasing cortisol enables better decision making.

As a final of desperation, The Jet starts 'to play possum' to confuse his opponent, which hilariously does work but concludes with the now aggressor landing a destructive flying knee on the weakened Urquidez.

By all accounts, actual contact was made between both players in particular a vicious cross in slow motion that Chan landed against the head of Urquidez that rocked the undefeated kickboxer. Thankfully, this did not translate to bad blood and the men would share a mutual respect for one another despite the hard hits.

At just under five minutes, this is still a tremendously impressive piece of action choreography and in many ways is still unmatched by most of what modern action cinema can furnish audiences with.

One would hope that Keanu Reeves opts to select this cinematic showing as a piece of masterclass in action for his upcoming documentary, on The Jet.

AUTHOR BIO
Vance Ang has primarily been professionally published in bodybuilding and fitness media since 2005, having written extensively for hardcopy publications such as Australian IRONMAN and FLEX; but also for e-publications such as RAW Muscle and also serving as a movie critic for the New York based FILM COMBAT SYNDICATE. He is a Melbourne based policy and strategy consultant currently undertaking his post graduate study in Law. In addition to bodybuilding and conservative politics, he has a keen interest in kicking based arts such as Savate, Sanda and Sikaran.

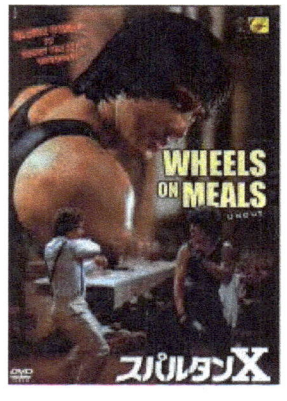
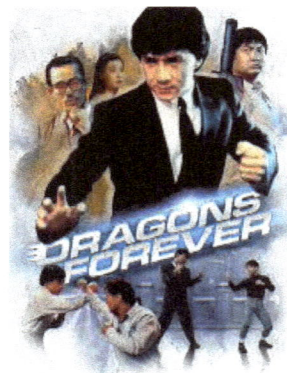

Offensive Action Toward Second Dan Grading

by Benjamin Ward

Martial arts provides a wealth of lessons to the martial artist and while becoming better at martial arts every day can't be tracked sometimes and progress can't be seen like: in The Matrix movies where Neo downloads martial arts into his brain through a computer and says "I know kung fu" instantaneously; it does happen.

Incremental advancements are made with each curious foray into its action. I say action as coming from a second dan (Ni-dan) belt grade while I work on mind-stuff, yaksuko, situational awareness, reactions, showmanship and learning and memorising the new grade kata for San-dan (third dan).

Second dan is a grading of action and fitness and like all gradings, a test. But it is so much more and produces so much more, even if it is only in training for it. Imagine you had no definitive career success, you didn't have 'the Big Four' (a house, a family, a car and a watch), perhaps you had a string of incomplete commitments or life just isn't what it once was. Ultimately, aside from these external motivators, imagine if you haven't had good values or virtue in your life... With Karate practice you have this even if it's the only thing. This is the environment that a dojo creates. You bow and you walk in with nothing but yourself and everyone is equal. The dojo is not full of advertising for this or that. It is a neutral space where you are called to action. And going into a training session, you at least have your action. The moment you start your action in your class, or your weightlifting session, flexibility exercises, kata, etc. you immediately have five virtuous qualities that are necessary to take action. You have respect, goal setting, patience, self-confidence, self-discipline. See diagram.

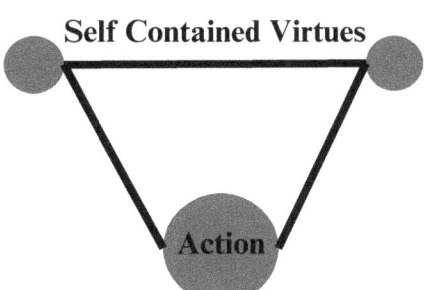

In a senjo, as it was in feudal Japan, the Shogun (grandmaster) had three right hand lieutenants, they were his Yakusa, Hatamoto and Yamabushi. These were represented by the colours RED, YELLOW and BLUE. In a modern senjo, the lieutenants are the higher up ranks in the style who represent aggression (RED/Yakusa), retreat and submission (YELLOW/Hatamoto) and Diplomacy/Neutrality and counter attacking strategy (BLUE/yamabushi). Interestingly, if we still were to use the pictorial representations of atomic structures as has been and is still used since the 20th century in modern physics; a Tungsten atom has the same structure of a senjo's arrangement of ranks and members surrounding the shogun; tungsten being the heaviest known metal on earth.

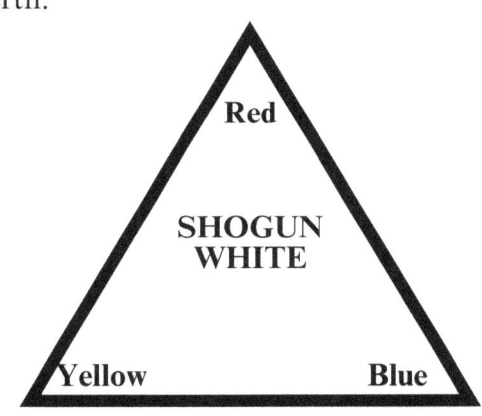

It is not uncommon for the Yakusa present in the senjo ceremony to be of a lower rank of second dan on the odd occasion standing surrounding the Shogun or head of the style. The Shogun encompasses the colour of white. The Shogun is white because he has passed through all the colours of lower ranks and methods of the martial art from each of the three trigrams qualities and lessons. He is now a combination of the three primary colours which in colour theory and the theory of ultra magnetic radiation on the light spectrum forms the colour white in a combination of all colours at the topmost end of the light range. All colours of light when combined form white light.

In a single dojo, the O kaicho or head sensei represents the Shogun and the assistant instructors and students as the shogunate. The way a dojo is run and directed at its main ethos comes from the head instructor. Whether the focus is to be the best fighter, to be a good person or in some pseudo dojos to use combat to get fit. The second dans will take a positive or offensive approach to this viewpoint, such as protesters against a government. Opposing viewpoints to an instructor's dojo may be found outside of the dojo in school, work, at a party, on the street by people with different ideological beliefs. The second dan is expected to aggressively or rather in this day and age positively and directly stand up for the dojo's beliefs. This is perhaps the only rank where a single colour permeates the ethos of the grading and rank.

A beginner student can display qualities of yakusa, hatamoto or yamabushi in greater predisposition and practice according to their individual self, but all students are expected to inherit the quality of yakusa (RED) for their second dan grading. In one style I practiced completing second dan grading was said to be entering the higher ranks of second dan and above called 'the league of blood'. Notice the red colour pronounced in this parochial tradition. Also, when the rank of second dan is achieved, the student gets red on the sleeves of their gi and red writing on their belt.

It is important to remember that, unlike the yakusa who are a criminal organisation in Japan. Becoming yakusa doesn't mean to be a rebel and think that the rules do not apply to you. While this is common of extremists in politics personality and training, ultimately it will come down to a more post-modern approach of directness and positivity in defending one's dojo ethos, i.e. to be a good person. In keeping this approach in mind second dan training and grading is unequivocally a grading of action and as mentioned in the introduction, to have action in the dojo or in practice contains five virtues: respect, goal setting, patience, self-confidence, self-discipline.

It is a physical grading, a martial arts marathon, as it is called. No time is spent on yaksuko applications and self-defence, no work is done on weapons training and although these elements are missing it teaches a karateka, the value of pure offensive action in a martial art petri dish bringing the most physical parts of a karate style. Whether it disgusts or delights, the karateka student and they stay a second dan for 10 years or readily embrace the approach of the third dan grading and all of its elements. It cannot be said it is a grading without virtue despite its offensive and direct nature. To be a modern day yakusa is to not lose ones principles or the principles of their dojo but to represent them passionately. Because for a person of offensive action, self-contained within their training, whether it is at the dojo or elsewhere, there is virtue.

Author Benjamin Ward

Karate No Rinrir

by Tim Nicklin

Today, Karate is a sport to most and a recreation to others and for a very few it's still a way of life, however karate started out as something completely different to what most see it to be today. Karate was not originally designed to be an international sports movement nor a money-making insurance business. Karate was and is a real fighting art (jissen karate jutsu) taught along ethical lines of ethics and meta-ethics (Rinri) how to act and why to act.

Me & my big brother Andrew

So what are ethics? Ethics are how we act and normative moral ethics are those ethics that govern our good or correct behaviour. Actions we use to deal with any situation in dealing with others in our society are our moral ethics. So, what then are meta-ethics? Meta-ethics rather than being our correct behaviour in actions and words (or otherwise actions in dealing with others) are the thought process that goes behind them in meta-ethics, we philosophize about the reasoning and rationale of ethics, we decide not only which actions are deemed good and therefore moral, but exactly why we think these are the correct actions or words to be used in any given situation.

So why is this important in Karate or any other martial arts? Because if we just do as we are told rather than understand why what we are being told is correct, we may never come to understand why one action is more morally correct than another. In Karate, it is perfectly acceptable to punch and kick someone in training or on the competition mats, however this is not acceptable behaviour once out in public, say in the schoolyard or in the workplace. Not only knowing this ethical point, but fully understanding it, gives us the ability to find our own moral compass and our own view on correct morally ethical behavior.

This is essential if we are going to study Karate or any other martial art or sport in any real depth.

Immanuel Kant in his work on the groundwork (1785) of ethics tells us that moral ethics must be a reaction to rational reason a priori to emotions and not a response to emotion of frustration or an inclination to emotion, but our ethical morals must be our duty to do the right thing all the time.

Karate was originally an Okinawan fighting art known as Toudi literally meaning Chinese hands. The people who trained in these arts were not peasants as commonly thought, neither were they just random members of the public. Karate or Toudi was taught to people of choice, people of standing in the community and the karate masters of those communities carefully taught only those they thought were suited with the correct character for karate, a character that could be trained to always do the correct moral action or speak the correct moral words in any given situation. Students either sought permission to study through family members or educational connection for reasons of health, self-improvement or similar. These people, as stated, had to be of good moral character.

These arts were taught in local villages and often comprised village dances and other rituals coming from both Te and Toudi. Okinawan arts were and still are steeped in local costumes and traditions by and large as an educational as well as fighting system, making it an effective all round martial art.

In 1392 the Ming Emperor sent 36 families from China to live on Okinawa Island, the idea was to help advance the Okinawans understandings in technology and diplomatic relations, including court conduct education (political ethics) when it came to the two countries dealing with each other. So, the idea of ethics being a part of martial arts has always been realized in Chinese Gung Fu.

In 1901 Ankō Itosu introduced Karate (Toudi) into the Okinawan school system, he believed this would result in strongly motivated students with high moral standards of ethics (precept 7 of Itosu -you must decide whether Karate is for health or to aid you in doing your duty).

Immanuel Kant described duty as the categorical imperative a moral law that not only are you happy to act upon yourself in your dealings with other, however you would be happy for all others to also act upon this moral law when dealing with you, making it a universal categorical imperative.
(Groundwork of the Metaphysics of Morals, Immanuel Kant, 1785).

So, we may deduce from this that the teaching of social ethics was intended to be a serious part of karate teachings, and therefore still should be. However, today apart from a short, much misunderstood bow (Ojigi or Rei) at the beginning of each class and maybe a nod to start your kata, ethics and much more importantly meta-ethics are missing from our Karate today, as they sadly are from our societies. Today we see more than ever the assaulting of the old and infirm, disrespect for law and order, whilst teachers stand afraid to teach in their classrooms. This is sadly a result of a breakdown in our moral fiber in our ethical behaviour.

I believe along with many others that Karate can be used (as originally intended) to teach new as well as existing students' strong moral values that would be a benefit to our societies, as well as teaching real and effective martial techniques. In fact, I would say the two should always go together as any uneducated thug can fight, but it takes a person of real moral value to purposely conduct him or herself morally correctly in a difficult situation.

Following on from teachers of the past, we could easily use Karate not just to create strong sports people with good sports motivation, but we could also help educate young people to become strong ethically minded people with a very high standard of moral ethics.

This could be achieved by adding moral conduct to our grading systems, rather than seeing this as a step away from tradition we could see it as a step back to moral tradition and we would be directly following in Ankō Itosu's footsteps if we started making moral conduct a condition for grading.
Karate no Kata (kata of karate) is about self-awareness as much as it is about self-motivation. That is what our Sensei is teaching us when he/she teaches kata in its traditional form away from sport and self-defence.

Anyone who has ever tried to seriously try to learn karate Kata in real depth will know the hard work that comes with the attitude of Mo Ichi Do (one more time), know what personal effort is at the end of the day, it's you that must find the effort no matter how much you Sensei helps with motivation, you must be the one to do the kata and you must want to do it for yourself, your own esteem first, because you are learning that if you can't find the effort to respect yourself you will never find the effort to respect others. This is character building of Karate kata, can you find what it takes to get back up there and start it all over again, can you find what it takes to do all the auxiliary training that goes with these kata, all this hard work being put by you into yourself builds character and that builds self-respect, self-esteem and that teaches us to respect others.

Learning to respect ourselves by learning the traditional kata of karate will not only provide an excellent sport for our young and an effective self-defense system for all, but much more importantly it will give us the inner strength and self-esteem to act with true moral ethic in all situations our life presents to us.

Respect comes from our self-esteem a sense of wellbeing about ourselves not just physically however far more importantly our mental health, if we feel good about ourselves if we feel we understand ourselves through our Karate training we can then project this feeling of wellbeing on to others as we interact with them during our daily lives. Meaning our Karate lessons and the conversations we have held in the dojo stay with us throughout our normal civilians lives our working or school day seven days a week, whether at church or at play we will always understand the correctly moral way to act, because we are never more than a few hours away from our next Karate lesson and a timely reminder on how to act correctly.

None of this is hard to achieve its just about being brave enough to take the time to ask yourself and your classmate what is the right thing to do in any given situation, that way we take our Karate classes with us into real life, and we can practice Karate as it should be practiced in everyday life with everyday minds (heijoshin). Karate is not just about hitting other people, as Chojun Migagi (founder of Goju Ryu) said, Karate is about not allowing others to hit you and not hitting others. That means it's more about ethics and meta-ethics than we realise today.

There must be a balance between the need to defend ourselves and tolerance for others, for if we tolerate other people's actions all the time, they will in turn become intolerant to us (Sir Karl Popper in Opens Society and its Enemies). So, by using moral ethics as a guide in our martial arts, as well as life, we should be better able to present ourselves in all situations.

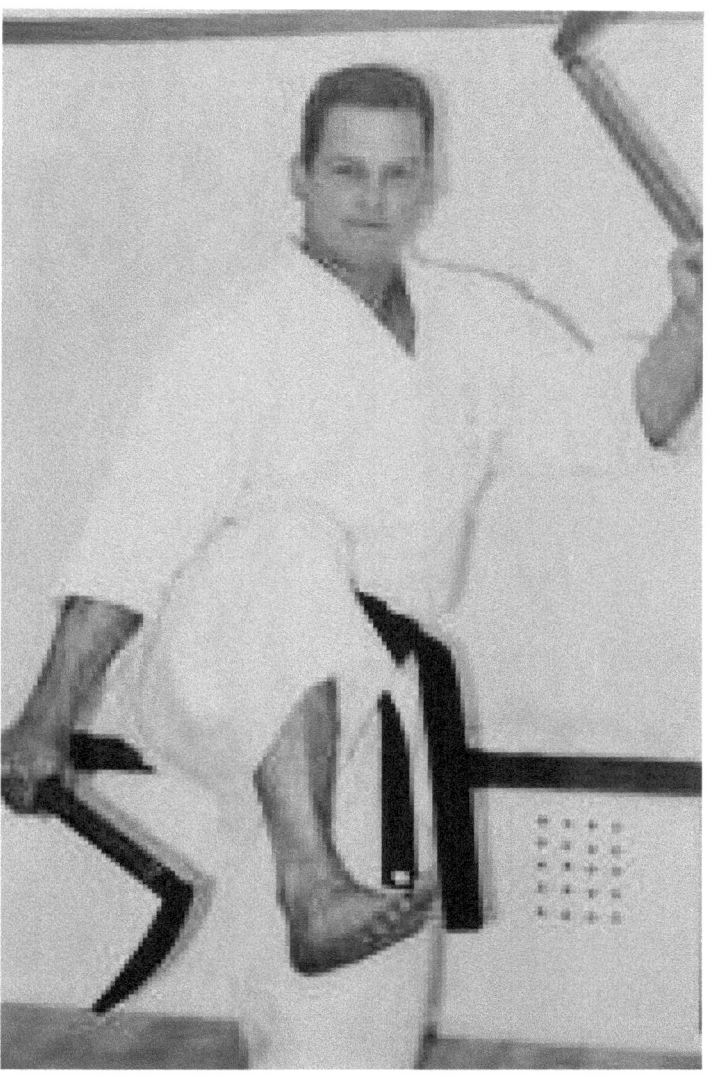

Tim Nicklin
7th Dan Niwa Dojo, Westen Australia

Reference
Kant, I. (1785). Groundwork of the Metaphysics of Morals. USA: Yale University Press.
Popper, K. (1945). The Opens Society and its Enemies. London: Rouledge

Mastering Kata: Techniques for Effective Learning and Understanding

by Maria Francis

Kata, or pre-arranged forms, are a fundamental aspect of many martial arts. They serve as a living encyclopedia of techniques, a tool for physical conditioning, and a means of preserving the art's history and philosophy. However, learning and remembering kata can be challenging, especially for beginners. Let's look at various techniques to help students effectively learn, remember, and understand kata.

Visualization and mental rehearsal are powerful tools for learning kata. By mentally practicing the movements, you can reinforce the sequence and identify areas that need improvement. To begin, find a quiet space and close your eyes. Visualize yourself performing the kata with perfect form and technique. Pay attention to details such as stances, transitions, and breathing. Incorporate mental rehearsal into your daily practice, even on days when you can't physically train. This technique enhances memory retention and deepens your understanding of the kata.

Bunkai, or application analysis, involves examining each movement within a kata to understand its practical purpose. By breaking the kata down into smaller sequences and exploring their potential applications, you can better grasp the meaning behind the movements. Research various interpretations of the kata and experiment with different scenarios. Apply your bunkai analysis during partner drills and self-defence practice. This process will help you internalize the kata's principles and make your performance more purposeful.

Mnemonic Devices and Storytelling Mnemonic devices are effective methods for remembering kata sequences. Create a story or narrative that links the kata's movements together. For example, imagine you are defending against multiple attackers in a specific environment. Assign each movement a role within the story, such as blocking a punch, counterattacking, or transitioning to a new position. Personalize your mnemonics to make them more memorable. Share your stories with training partners to reinforce your learning and gain new perspectives.

Partner Work and Cooperative Learning: to practice kata with a partner offers many benefits. Mirror each other's movements to identify and correct discrepancies in technique. Perform synchronization drills to develop timing and rhythm. Provide constructive feedback to help each other improve. When facing difficult sections of the kata, collaborate to problem-solve and find solutions. Partner work enhances accountability, motivation, and the overall learning experience.

Rhythm, Timing, and Musical Association: rhythm and timing are essential elements of kata performance. Use counting, breathing, or musical cues to maintain a consistent rhythm throughout the kata. Explore how different tempos affect your power, balance, and transitions. Associate specific kata movements with musical phrases or beats to create a memorable soundtrack. This approach can make practice more engaging and help you internalize the kata's flow.

Writing out the moves of a kata offers several advantages for martial arts practitioners. By physically writing down the sequence of moves, you engage multiple senses and learning pathways, reinforcing the information in your memory and making it easier to recall the kata later. This process also helps you better understand how the movements connect and flow together, highlighting areas where you may be uncertain or need additional practice. As you write, you can make notes about key aspects of each movement, such as stance, body alignment, or breathing, ensuring that you are performing each technique correctly.

Having a written record of the kata serves as a valuable reference tool, allowing you to review specific sections or teach the kata to others. The process of writing encourages deep thinking about each movement and its purpose, leading to new insights, ideas for bunkai (applications), or personal interpretations of the kata. A clear, written description of the kata improves communication and teaching, making it easier to guide students or training partners.

Kata mapping is a technique that involves creating a visual representation of a kata's movements, usually as a diagram or a flowchart. This approach offers a unique way to analyse and understand the structure, flow, and key elements of a kata. By mapping out the kata, practitioners can gain a clearer picture of how the movements connect, identify patterns, and uncover potential applications.

To create a kata map, begin by breaking the kata down into its individual movements or sequences. Each movement can be represented by a box or symbol, with arrows indicating the direction of the technique and the transitions between movements. Different colours or shapes can denote specific types of techniques, such as strikes, kicks, blocks, or stances.

As you map out the kata, pay attention to any recurring patterns or combinations of techniques. These patterns may reveal underlying strategies or principles within the kata. Consider the spatial relationships between movements, such as changes in direction or distance from an imagined opponent.

Kata mapping can also be used to explore bunkai (applications) by visualizing how each movement could be applied in a self-defence scenario. By mapping out the kata with potential applications in mind, practitioners can discover new interpretations and gain a deeper understanding of the kata's practical value.

Once complete, a kata map serves as a visual aid for learning, teaching, and analysing the kata. It can help practitioners memorize the sequence of movements, identify areas for improvement, and communicate their understanding of the kata to others. Kata maps can also be shared and compared with others, fostering discussions and the exchange of ideas within your dojo.

Incorporating kata mapping into your training routine can provide a fresh perspective on familiar katas and enhance your overall understanding of the art. By visually representing the kata's structure and flow, you can uncover new insights, refine your technique, and deepen your appreciation for the depth and complexity of the martial arts.

Mastering kata is a lifelong journey that requires patience, dedication, and a willingness to explore various learning methods. By incorporating techniques such as visualization, bunkai analysis, mnemonic devices, partner work, rhythm, and creative exploration, you can enhance your kata performance and understanding. Remember, consistent practice is key. Embrace the process, experiment with different approaches, and find what works best for you. As you deepen your connection with kata, you'll not only improve your physical skills but also cultivate discipline, self-awareness, and a greater appreciation for the art.

Write for Us

We want your authentic story, your journey and the reason WHY you love what you do. Below is a list of suggested topics. It is not exhaustive, so if you have an idea that we haven't come up with yet, drop us a line: training tips; technique workshops; style origins;kids in ma; training fuel; style anatomy; family pages; instructor profile; keeping it real; and more...

We are a quarterly magazine that celebrates and inspires a broad community of Martial Artists across the country. Our goal is to support all MA practitioners. Both instructors and students are encouraged to share their personal experiences, triumphs, and challenges within the style they love.

We feature interviews, rants, research, photography, projects and editorials that are respectful to all styles and are keeping in line with our magazine's inclusive philosophy.

Just as no two styles of Martial Arts are alike, our writers should have their own unique voice and tell their story from their own perspective. We encourage you to speak your truth.

Don't worry if you feel that your writing is not up to scratch, just tell us your story, your tip or your instruction the best way you can and our in-house editor will do the rest.

Email your submissions to info@martialartsmagazineaustralia.com (text in .doc) and (photos in JPEG).

www.ingramcontent.com/pod-product-compliance
Lightning Source LLC
Chambersburg PA
CBHW061759290426
44109CB00030B/2895